PZ-2

Written by The Puzzle House
Designed by Chalk & Cheese

tangerine Press™

Copyright © 2001 Top That! Publishing plc
Published by Tangerine Press ™,
an imprint of Scholastic Inc.
555 Broadway, New York, NY 10012.
All rights reserved.

1 MOSAIC

Fit the letter tiles back into the frame.
When the tiles fit together in the right order,
the mosaic has FIVE words reading across,
and FOUR words reading down.

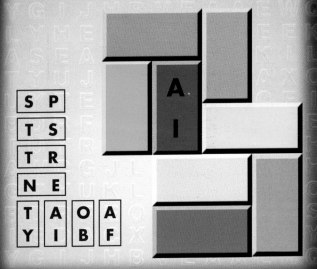

2 AFTER–WORDS

Which word can go after all these words to
make new words?

FRIEND _____

SPACE _____

WAR _____

BEEP BEEP!

Emma's new watch gives an amazingly loud beep every time a 3 appears. It is 24-hour clock; 0800 is 8 am, 1200 is noon and 1300 is 1 pm and so on. Each minute a new set of four digits is displayed. If two 3s appear at the same time there would be two beeps and if three 3s appeared there would be three beeps.

How many beeps will there be between 08.00 and 09.00?

OFF LINE

Remove three lines to be left with a pattern of exactly FOUR squares.

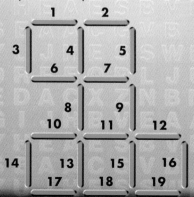

5 ON GUARD

Find a way through the passageway without coming across a guard.

6 SECRET SEVEN

Rearrange the letters in the word below to make another word of seven letters.

ASSUAGE
_ _ _ _ _ _ _ .

CLUE
Think HOT DOG

BRUSH STOKES

How many brushes are pictured here?

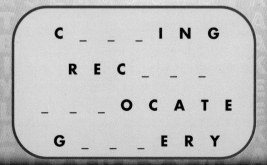

MIND THE GAP

What three-letter word completes all of the following words?

C _ _ _ I N G

R E C _ _ _

_ _ _ O C A T E

G _ _ _ E R Y

QUARTERBACK

A word square reads the same across and down. Fit the listed words back to make four word squares each containing four words. One word is in position to start you off.

AVOW
DARK
DELL
EVIL
HIVE
IDEA
KIND
LOVE
NEAR
OGRE
PEEK
PEWS
SHED
SLAP
SOUP
URGE

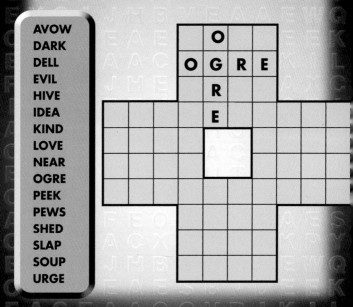

SPLITZER

Rearrange this row of ten letters into two five-letter words which are the names of body organs. The words read from left to right and the letters are in the correct order.

H L E I A V R E R T

TRIANGLE TEST

How many triangles are in this pattern?

HONEYCOMB

Each answer contains six letters and is written in the six spaces that link together around a number. Answers always go in a clockwise direction and every first letter is in place. When the honeycomb is complete the inner ring of six letters will spell out a star sign.

1 Old fashioned sea bandit.

2 People protecting or watching over a place.

3 Rough and tough.

4 Unlawful killing.

5 Season of the year.

6 Metal fastening bolts.

13

BACK WORDS

Solve the clues: the second answer is the first answer written backwards.

GIVE MONEY ∗ HIGH-PITCHED BARK

_ _ _ _   ∗   _ _ _ _

14

MORE OR LESS

Which is greater, the number of hours in three days, or the number of eggs in five and a half dozen?

OR

15

ADDER

Join two separate words to create a new word.

ORGAN OF HEARING _ _ _

+ FALSE HAIR _ _ _

= INSECT _ _ _ _ _ _

CREATURE CODE

In this code, symbols have been used to take the place of letters of the alphabet. The first group spells out the word RAT. Can you work out the other coded creatures

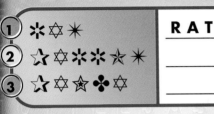

1) ❊ ✩ ✳
2) ☆ ✩ ❊ ❊ ✩ ✳
3) ☆ ✩ ✩ ♣ ✩

✩	✢	✣	✤	✥	♣	♦	✧	★	☆	✪	✫	✬
A	B	C	D	E	F	G	H	I	J	K	L	M
✭	✮	✯	✱	✲	✳	✴	✵	❊	✶	✷	❋	✺
N	O	P	Q	R	S	T	U	V	W	X	Y	Z

RAT
_____
_____
_____

LINKS

Which word will go after the first word and before the second word?

AIR _ _ _ _ HOLE

SECRET SEVEN

Rearrange the letters in the word below to make another word of seven letters.

WOBLERS
_____

_ _ _ _ _ _ _

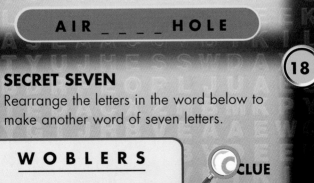

CLUE
Think SPORTS MAN

PICTURE GALLERY

Use the clues to find the portrait of
Sir Jasper Murgatroyd.

- Sir Jasper has a black moustache.
- Sir Jasper wears a hat.
- Sir Jasper has a beard.
- Sir Jasper has a scar on his left cheek.
- Sir Jasper has large, bushy eyebrows.

GIVE ME FIVE

Solve the clues, so that each answer contains five letters. Write all the answers in place, and the shaded squares reading down will reveal the name of a musical instrument.

1. Opposite of last
2. Outer covering of an egg
3. Sailing boat
4. Bad weather
5. To set alight
6. Push this to power a bicycle
7. Meadow
8. Number in a trio

CARD TRICK

How do you turn something RAW into a card game?

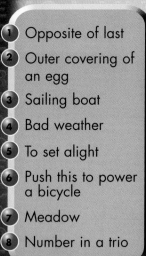

LOTS OF SPOTS

Using the words listed, make three word squares which read the same across and down. The word SPOT appears in each square.

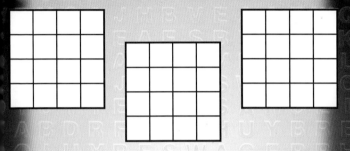

DODO, DROP, ETNA, ISLE, LOAN, ODDS, OVAL, PAVE, SPOT, SPOT, SPOT, TELL

TOP TEN

Complete the word by filling the spaces with a whole number between ONE and TEN.

E X _ _ _ D

WHAT'S NEXT?

What is the next letter to go in the space?

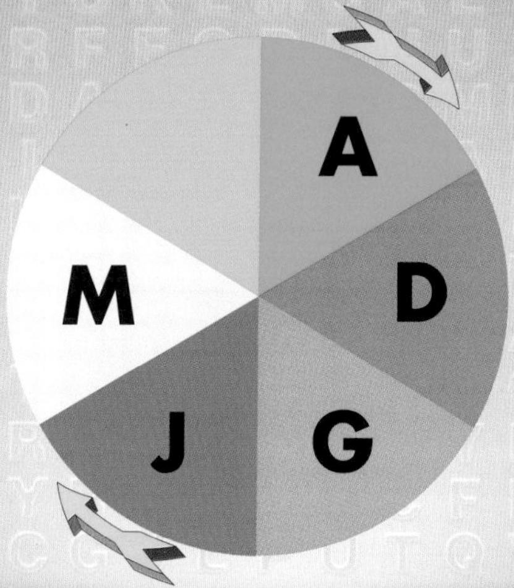

A

D

M

G

J

ANIMAL–FILL

Think of the name of a creature that will fill in the spaces and complete the name of another creature.

P _ _ _ H E R

TREE SURGERY

Can you unscramble the groups of letters to spell out different parts of a tree?

1. **R A K B** _____

2. **S O R T O** _____

3. **R A N C H B** _____

4. **F A L E** _____

5. **T N R U K** _____

SPLITZER

Arrange this row of ten letters into two five-letter words which are the names of birds.
The words read from left to right and the letters are in the correct order.

E A G A G L O O E S E

/ _____

BLOCKS

Can you fit the blocks below back to read the message?

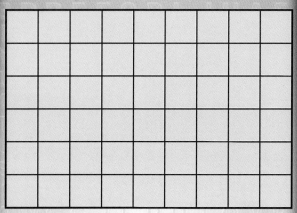

ON LINE

Add one line to complete each letter and spell out a high tech item.

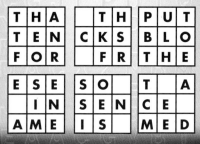

NICE MICE

Solve each clue and write the answers into the spaces in the grid. All answers have four letters. Put the first letter in the outer circle, then move towards the center. Only one letter changes between answers, and answer 8 will be only one letter different from answer 1.

1 Scurrying creatures.
2 Food often eaten with a Chinese meal.
3 Speed contest.
4 Part of the body with nose, eyes, and mouth.
5 Price for a ticket to travel.
6 Flames and smoke.
7 A folder in which to keep papers.
8 Measure of distance.

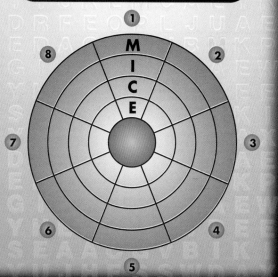

31

LINKS

Which word will go after the first word and before the second word?

BLUE _ _ _ _ _ SHARK

32

ON TARGET

Which three numbers will have to be hit to make exactly 80?

17

15   39   23

24

AFTER-WORDS

Which word can go after all these words to make new words?

D E A D _____

L I F E _____

O N _____

NUMBER-RING

Move around the circle. You have to write a number in the blank section that will continue the number pattern.

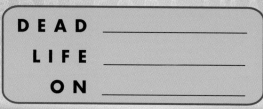

23

3

18

13

8

SECRET SEVEN

Rearrange the letters in the word below to make another word of seven letters.

BOREDOM

_ _ _ _ _ _ _

CLUE

Think IN THE HOUSE

PAIRS

Which two badges are exactly alike?

1 **2**

3 **4**

5 **6**

MIND THE GAP

What three-letter word completes all of the following words?

D E _ _ _ E

_ _ _ C H

_ _ _ T E R Y

_ _ _ T L E

MORE OR LESS

What is more, the number of sides in nine triangles, or the number of sides in four octagons?

x 9   OR   x 4

BACK WORDS

Solve the clues: the second answer
is the first answer written backwards.

HOLE IN THE GROUND ✳ UPPER EDGE

___ ___ ___ ✳ ___ ___ ___

40

SNAKES ALIVE!

The name of a type of snake is hidden in
each of the sentences below. Find them
by joining words or parts of words
together.

1 How sad Derek looks.

2 They stayed all night at their
daughter's disco, bravely in my opinion.

3 The Jumbo arrived on time.

HAPPY BIRTHDAY

Jennifer was 15 yesterday.

Next year she will be 17.

What is the date of Jennifer's birthday, and on which date would the first two things have been true?

_____

NATIONWIDE

Rearrange the letters in the words below to spell out the names of countries.

① **PURE**

② **PAINS**

③ **PANEL**

④ **ENEMY**

ADDER

Join two separate words to create a new word.

LIMB   _ _ _
+ FINISH   _ _ _
= OLD STORY   _ _ _ _ _ _

FACE FACTS

Use the letters that make up the face to make a name.

SECRET SEVEN

Rearrange the letters in the word below to make another word of seven letters.

BOLSTER

 CLUE

Think SHELLFISH

_ _ _ _ _ _ _

NIGHT SIGNS

Shapes and signs have been used to take the place of letters of the alphabet. Can you work out what the words are? They are all night creatures and the first word is OWL.

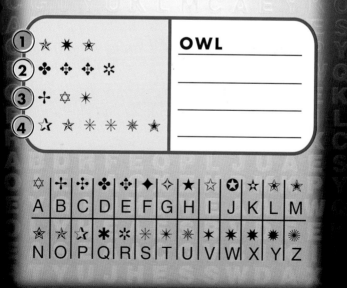

1) ☆ ✳ ☆
2) ✤ ✜ ✤ ✳
3) ✛ ✡ ✳
4) ☆ ✬ ✳ ✳ ✳ ★

OWL
_____
_____
_____

✡	✛	✜	✤	✣	◆	✧	★	☆	✪	☆	✳	✬
A	B	C	D	E	F	G	H	I	J	K	L	M

✬	✬	✰	✱	✲	✳	✴	✵	✶	✷	✸	✹	✺
N	O	P	Q	R	S	T	U	V	W	X	Y	Z

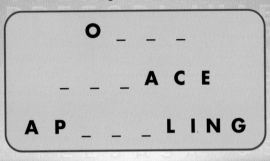

47

MIND THE GAP
What three-letter word completes all of the following words?

O _ _ _

_ _ _ A C E

A P _ _ _ L I N G

48

LINKS
Which word will go after the first word and before the second word?

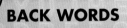

R A I N _ _ _ T I E

49

BACK WORDS
Solve the clues: the second answer is the first answer written backwards.

PAN   *   SUMMIT

_ _ _   *   _ _ _

ON THE MAP

Here are four sketch maps of this scene.
Only one is correct in every detail.
Which one is it?

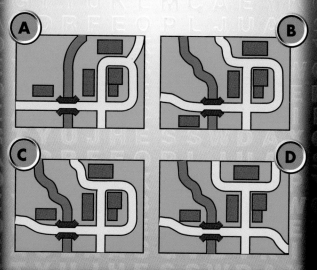

A

B

C

D

51

SQUASHED SANDWICHES!

Can you unscramble the groups of letters to spell out the names of sandwich fillings?

1. CEEEHS
2. AUNT
3. CKENCHI
4. KRTEUY
5. MHA

52

SECRET SEVEN

Rearrange the letters in the word below to make another word of seven letters.

PRECAST

_ _ _ _ _ _ _

CLUE

Think
FLOOR COVERINGS

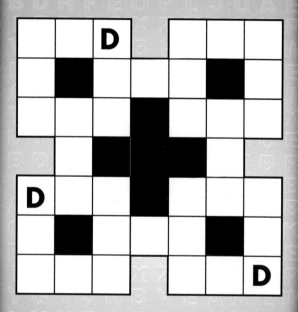

3D

With three Ds in place, can you fit all these three–letter words back into the frame?

AGE ALL ASH ASP AXE BAD

BOA DOE DUO DYE ELF END

FOX GNU HUT LID OFF OWL

POT YES

PATTERN PLAY
Which pattern is not like the others?

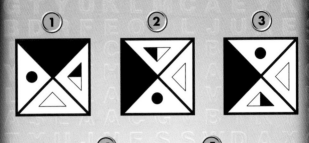

ADDER
Join two separate words to create a new word.

OVERWEIGHT _ _ _

+ NOT HIM _ _ _

= DAD _ _ _ _ _ _

STARGAZER

All answers contain four letters and follow the direction shown by the arrows.

1. Pastry containing sweet or creamy filling
2. Light froth on the surface of a liquid
3. The movement of water
4. Wild dog-like animal
5. Place where crops are grown
6. Give notice of danger

COMPUTER CODE

Shapes and signs have been used to take the place of letters of the alphabet. Can you work out what word each group makes? There is an alphabet below to help you.

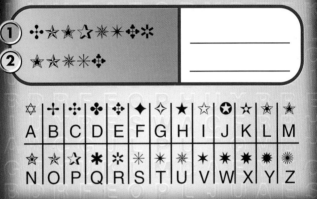

✡	✝	✢	♣	✤	◆	✧	★	✩	✪	✫	✬	✭
A	B	C	D	E	F	G	H	I	J	K	L	M

✮	✯	✰	✱	✲	✳	✴	✵	✶	✷	✸	✹	✺
N	O	P	Q	R	S	T	U	V	W	X	Y	Z

MIND THE GAP

What three-letter word completes all of the following words?

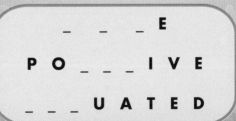

_ _ _ E

P O _ _ _ I V E

_ _ _ U A T E D

LEMON-AID

How many times does the word LEMON appear in the box of letters? It can read in any direction as a straight line of letters.

AFTER–WORDS

Which word can go after all these words to make new words?

CODE _____

CROSS _____

PASS _____

61 ROUNDABOUT

Find a pathway that leads to the center of the maze.

62 LINKS

Which word will go after the first word and before the second word?

TREASURE _ _ _ _ _ NUT

EUROPEAN CAPITALS

The name of a European capital city is hidden in each of the sentences below. Find them by joining words or parts of words.

1 She gets mad riding behind slow moving traffic.

2 Grandpa risked great danger during the war it seems.

3 Taking a deep breath ensures you're then ready for anything.

4 I took the toy from Emily and gave it to her sister.

5 I was sure that I recognised the blond onlooker.

6 The number line dancing has increased out of all proportion.

FRUITY

Take half of a PEAR.

Add the middle of a GRAPE.

Add one third of a CHERRY.

Which fruit do you have?

WHAT AM I?

My first is in stiff
But isn't in fish.

My second's in dash
But isn't in dish.

My third is in bread
But isn't in dear.

My fourth is in feel
But isn't in fear.

My fifth's not in fowl,
Though you'll find it in few.
You'll make the discovery
If you follow it through.

MORE OR LESS?

What is more, the number of days in
May doubled or the number of fortnights
in two years?

MAY

						1
2	3	4	5	6	7	8
9	10	11	12	13	14	15
16	17	18	19	20	21	22
23	24	25	26	27	28	29
30	31					

OR

ALPHA-NUMBERS

The groups of letters are arranged in alphabetical order. Move them around to spell out different numbers.

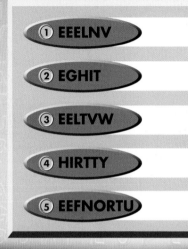

1. EEELNV

2. EGHIT

3. EELTVW

4. HIRTTY

5. EEFNORTU

SPLITZER

This row of ten letters can be split into two five-letter words which are the names of two types of boat. Words read from left to right and the letters are in the correct order. What are they?

C A Y A C N O H E T

/

FAST TRACK

Four athletes have run races.
They have run different distances, and all
finished in different positions. Can you figure
out each person's name, his or her event, and
finishing position?

BACK WORDS

Solve the clues: the second answer is the
first answer written backwards.

RODENT   *   BLACK LIQUID

_ _ _ _   *   _ _ _ _

IN THE MIDDLE

Put a letter in each of the sets of brackets which can be added to the end of the first word and the start of the second word. The letters used will read down to spell out a fruit.

> T O O (_) A N D
> F A R (_) Y E S
> F I R (_) E A T
> H E R (_) P E N
> L A W (_) E A R

YOUR DEAL

You have been dealt four playing cards that are all Hearts.

The cards have consecutive numbers.

The four cards add up to 26.

Which cards have you been dealt?

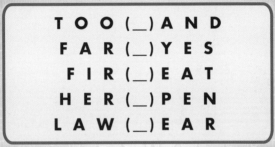

COMPU-COMMAND

Add one line to complete each letter and spell out a computer command.

MOONS

Here are two moons. The first shows a moon against the night sky, the second shows a moon when it has been eclipsed so it appears as a dark object against a light sky. Which moon is the bigger of the two?

TOP TEN

Complete the word by filling the spaces with a whole number between ONE and TEN.

F E M I _ _ _ _ _

NUMBER-RING

Start from the arrow and move around the circle. You have to write a number in the blank section that will continue the number pattern.

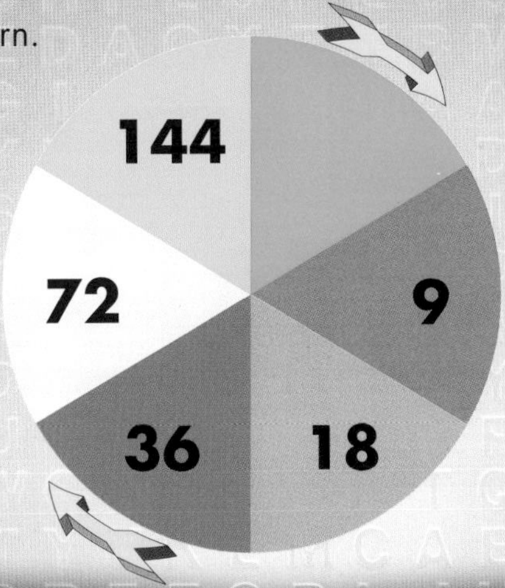

144

72

9

36

18

ADDER

Join two words to create a new word.

NOT ON _ _ _
+ FROZEN WATER _ _ _
= PLACE OF WORK _ _ _ _ _ _

NUMBER FIT

Fit all the numbers back into the frame.

3 DIGITS | 112 253 317 446 511 592 644 708 826 909

4 DIGITS | 1177 1261 1463 1859 1902 2245 3032 3913
4420 5015 5201 6300 6377 7678 8094 9684

5 DIGITS | 10803 27599 31728 73381

6 DIGITS | 125630 253618 312080 462926 482572
573054 771488 890101

7 DIGITS | 2968022 4373676 7222222
8117923 8835440 9052351

FACE FACTS

Use the letters that make up the face to make a name.

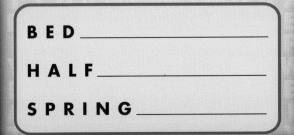

AFTER–WORDS

Which word can go after all these words to make new words?

B E D _____

H A L F _____

S P R I N G _____

81

DOMINOES

There is something that links all the dominoes shown here. What should appear in the last domino to keep the link going?

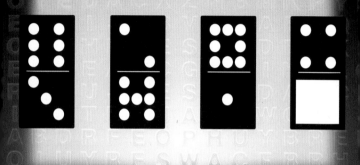

82

MIND THE GAP

What three-letter word completes all of the following words?

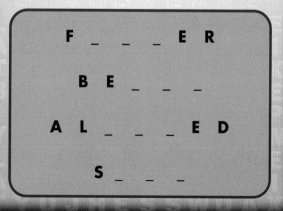

F _ _ _ E R

BE _ _ _

AL _ _ _ E D

S _ _ _

SECRET SEVEN

Rearrange the letters in the word below to make another word of seven letters.

LACEUPS

_ _ _ _ _ _ _

CLUE

Think SPACESHIP

TRI-PATH

Which path contains most triangles?

A   B   C   D   E

SIDEWAYS

What is more, the number of sides in three rectangles, or the number of sides in two pentagons?

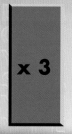

x 3   **x 2**

LASSO

There are seven warriors on the screen. You need to make sure they can't get to each other. You have three circular force shields like the one shown. How can you position them so that every warrior is trapped alone?

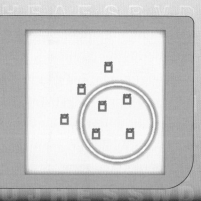

ORANGE PEEL

Solve the clues. Each answer contains the same letters, plus or minus one letter.

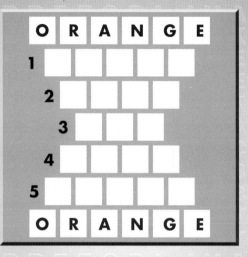

| | O | R | A | N | G | E |

1. Rifle shooting gallery
2. A bell sounded
3. Piece of cloth
4. Camping equipment
5. Bad temper

LINKS

Which word will go after the first word and before the second word?

NAVY _ _ _ _ JEANS

89

SPLITZER

This row of ten letters can be split into two five-letter words which are the names of two things used to make buildings. Words read from left to right and the letters are in the correct order. What are they?

B R S I T O C K N E

/ _____

90

MUSIC BOX

Use each letter in the box to name a musical instrument.

O	N	P
S	H	X
E	A	O

ADDER

Join two separate words to create
a new word.

**OPPOSITE
OF AGAINST**   _ _ _

+ OBTAIN   _ _ _

= FAIL TO REMEMBER   _ _ _ _ _ _

WHAT'S NEXT?

What is the next letter to go in the space?

MIND THE GAP

What three-letter word completes
all of the following words?

H _ _ _ E R

CH _ _ _ I N G

TR _ _ _ S

HANDY

At the end of a show, eight children form a
line at the front of the stage. As they bow to
the audience they hold hands. How many
hands are touching?

SECRET SEVEN

Rearrange the letters in the word below to make another word of seven letters.

H A R I C O T

_ _ _ _ _ _ _

CLUE

Think
HORSE DRAWN

BLOCKBACK

Fit the nine blocks back into the grid to form a completed crossword in which words interlock going either across or down.

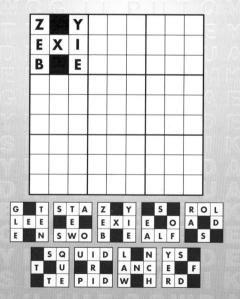

BACK WORDS

Solve the clues: the second answer is the first answer written backwards.

NOT COOKED $*$ SERIES OF BATTLES

_ _ _ _ $*$ _ _ _ _

ROULETTE

Arrange the numbers on the roulette wheel to fill the center circle and outer sections. Each diagonal of three numbers, always including the center number, must add up to exactly 20. No consecutive numbers can be touching in sections of the outer wheel.

3   4   5   6   7   8   9

AFTER-WORDS

Which word can go after all these words to make new words?

B A C K _____

C O L L A R _____

W I S H _____

CENTURY

Victoria is 100 years old. She's been made a special cake with 100 candles on it. Each candle will burn for exactly 3 minutes. It takes two seconds to light each candle. If there's just one person lighting the candles, will any candles have gone out by the time the hundredth is lit?

101 BACK WORDS

Solve the clues: the second answer is the first answer written backwards.

SWEET POTATO * FIFTH MONTH

_ _ _   *   _ _ _

102 ABC

There is only one line that does not contain each of the letters A, B, and C. Which one is it?

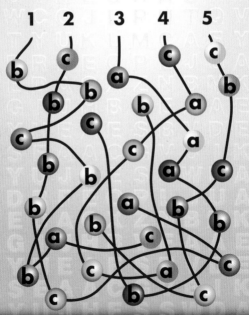

SECRET SEVEN

Rearrange the letters in the words below to make another word of seven letters.

CLOSE - UP

CLUE

Think PAIRS

_ _ _ _ _ _ _

HAPPY FAMILIES

Mr. and Mrs. Smith have five daughters.

Each of the daughters has one brother.

The entire family lives in the same house.

How many people live in the Smith house?

(105)

MIND THE GAP

Which single three-letter word completes all of the following words.

_ _ _ W A R D

B E _ _ _ E

_ _ _ G E D

I N _ _ _ M A T I O N

(106)

FACE FACTS

Use the letters that make up the face to make a name.

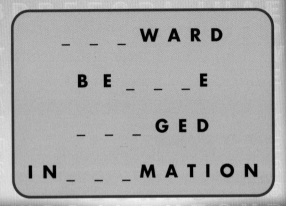

AFTER-WORDS
Which word can go after all these words to make new words?

B I R T H _____

S U N _____

W E E K _____

ADDER
Join two separate words to create a new word.

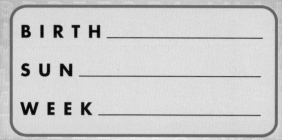

YOUNG GOAT _ _ _
+ SHORT SLEEP _ _ _
= HOLD FOR RANSOM _ _ _ _ _ _

LINKS
Which word will go after the first word and before the second word?

WATER _ _ _ JUMP

ALPHA-SEARCH

A word square reads the same whether you read it across or down. Use all these EIGHT words to make TWO word squares.

ALSO
DOOM
ENDS
GLAD
IRON
LILO
LIME
MOOD

NUMBER-RING

Move around the circle. You have to write a number in the blank section that will continue the number pattern.

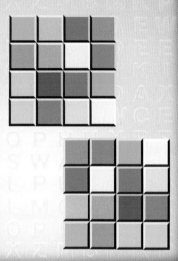

90
94
100
97
99

PICK A WORD

WAX MOTTO TOMATO

All these words have something in common. One word from the list below shares that something. Which word is it?

CHEESE HARM TOOTH VERTICAL

CUBA

A cube is a solid shape with six sides. All these patterns contain six joined sides. No matter how hard you try, it would be impossible to construct a solid cube from most of the patterns. There's one shape that could be used to form a cube. Which one is it?

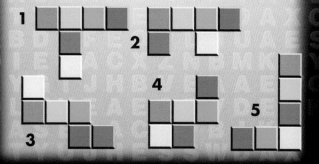

ALPHA-SEARCH

Search for the letters that aren't there! Each letter appears once, but five do not appear at all. Find the missing letters, then arrange them to spell out the name of a wild animal.

D H J O M P Y
I T G L C V S F
X W K Q U N

Animal Name

_____

115

LOTSA LEGS

Five cowboys are looking after a herd of cattle. If there are 150 legs altogether, how many cattle are there?

SPLITZER

This row of ten letters can be split into two five-letter words which are the names of two means of transport. Words read from left to right and the letters are in the correct order. What are they?

| T | R | T | R | U | A | I | C | N | K |

/
_____

ALL CHANGE

Solve the clues and turn the top word into the bottom one. Change just one letter with each new word.

① Person forced to work for someone else		**S L A V E**
② Remove hair or stubble from a man's face		_____
③ Push		_____
④ Land by the sea		_____
⑤ Boring and unpleasant task		_____
⑥ Group of notes played together		**C H O R D**

MATCHING WORD

Which word can go before all these words?

① _____ **BOARD**

② _____ **RACE**

③ _____ **SHOES**

④ _____ **WATER**

⑤ _____ **OUT**

BACK WORDS

Solve the clues: the second answer is the first answer written backwards.

SKETCH ✳ **HOSPITAL**

_ _ _ _ _ ✳ _ _ _ _ _

PYRAMID

Fit all the words back into the pyramid grid. Each word is written in a mini-pyramid shape. The first letter of each word goes in a numbered space. The second letter goes in the space directly above, the third letter goes to the right, and the fourth letter goes to the left. The word KNEE is in place to give you the idea.

BRAG **HERE** **INKY** **KEEN** **KNEE** **NICE**
OGRE **PAIR** **SARI** **SCAR** **SIGN** **STYE**
TREE **WEEK** **WENT**

WHAT'S NEXT?

What is the next letter to go in the space?

M

T

W

T

F

SECRET SEVEN

Rearrange the letters in the word below to make another word of seven letters.

CRUELTY

CLUE

Think
KNIVES AND FORKS

RHYMER

My first is in cheat
And also in harm.
My second's in wear
But isn't in warm.
My third is in mat
But isn't in meet.
My fourth is in three
But isn't in heat.
My fifth is in true,
But isn't in love.
There's a clue for you there
In the words up above.

ON LINE

Add one line to complete each letter and spell out a high tech item.

AFTER-WORDS

Which word can go after all these words to make new words?

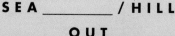

SEA _____ / HILL _____

OUT _____

126 BLANKS

Work out the pattern of numbers then fill in the blanks.

1 2 2 ▲ 4 4 △ 8 8 △ __

6   12   24   __

127 ADDER

Join two separate words to create a new word.

EQUIPMENT   _ _ _

+ NUMBER   _ _ _

= YOUNG CAT   _ _ _ _ _ _

128 MIND THE GAP

What three-letter word completes all of the following words?

```
_ _ _ T E R
  O R _ _ _
H A _ _ _ A T
  _ _ _ E
```

MIRROR IMAGE

Here's a message as it would appear if ordinary writing was viewed in a mirror. However, on reflection, there's one letter that is not shown as an accurate mirror image. Which one is it?

WHICH LETTER IS NOT SHOWN CORRECTLY HERE?

ON SONG

Use the words below to make two word squares. Each square must contain the word SONG.

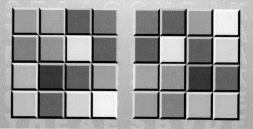

GLEE HISS INTO NAME
OVAL SONG SONG STUN

131

FACE FACTS

Use the letters that make up the face to make a name.

H
R
L
A
E

_____

132

TOP TEN

Complete the word by filling in the spaces with a whole number between ONE and TEN.

A N Y _ _ _

MIDDLE MOVES

Each clue has two answers. The two answer words are spelled the same except that the middle letters are different.

1 Camp bed ★ Slice with a knife (3 letters)

ANSWERS _____

2 With frozen water on the surface ★ Climbing or creeping plant (3 letters)

ANSWERS _____

3 Strike with a bat ★ Really warm (3 letters)

ANSWERS _____

4 An enclosed area in a building for a horse ★ Without moving (5 letters)

ANSWERS _____

5 Section of a book ★ Noisy talk (7 letters)

ANSWERS _____

LINKS

Which word will go after the first word and before the second word?

EGG _ _ _ _ _ FISH

TRUE OR FALSE?

The Angel family have three boys named Andy, Bob, and Carl. Their neighbors, the De Villes, also have three boys called Andy, Bob, and Carl.

The Angel family always tell the truth.

The De Villes always lie.

Three boys are playing together.
Two are De Villes the other is an Angel.
There is an Andy, a Bob, and a Carl, but from which family?

Boy 1 said that his name was not Bob.

Boy 2 said that his name was not Andy.

Boy 3 said that his name was Andy.

Can you figure out the last names of these three boys?

① **Boy 1** _____

② **Boy 2** _____

③ **Boy 3** _____

SPLITZER

This row of ten letters can be split into two five-letter words which are the names of two parts of a house. Words read from left to right and the letters are in the correct order. What are they?

A F T L T I O C O R

/
_____

NUMBER RING

Move around the circle. You have to write a number in the blank section that will continue the number pattern

1

3

9

27

81

138 BACK WORDS

Solve the clues: the second answer
is the first answer written backwards.

FAWN ✱ **GRASS**

_ _ _ _   ✱   _ _ _ _ _

139 AFTER-WORDS

Which word can go after all these words to
make new words?

BREAK _____

COUNT _____

TOUCH _____

140 SECRET SEVEN

Rearrange the letters in the word below to
make another word of seven letters.

CASTERS

_ _ _ _ _ _ _

CLUE

Think FILM STARS

3-4-5

Fit all the listed words back into the frame.

3 Letters ARM AXE END HAS ICE MEN TEA TIP

4 Letters ACHE ARMY DEEP DIET EAST IDEA MELT MIND

5 Letters ALIVE ANNUL CIVIC DUVET DWELL ELDER ENVOY EXCEL GLOOM GRAND IDIOT INCUR INDEX OUNCE RHYME TALLY TOTAL VICAR

ADDER

Join two separate words to create a new word.

NOISE OF A COW

+ DANGER COLOR
_____

= A SECURED BOAT

_ _ _ _

+ _ _ _ _ _
_____

= _ _ _ _ _ _ _

MIND THE GAP

What three-letter word completes all of the following words?

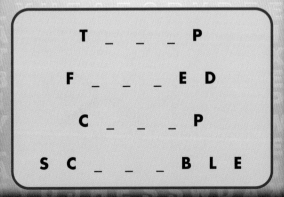

T _ _ _ P

F _ _ _ E D

C _ _ _ P

S C _ _ _ B L E

OH BOY!

Rearrange the letters in the words below to spell out boy's names

① **EDNA** _____

② **RESENT** _____

③ **SINNED** _____

TOP OF THE HEAP

Can you pick up the sticks so you always take the top one off the pile?

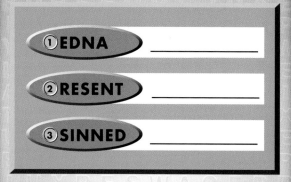

ANSWERS

1 **MOSAIC**

2 **AFTER-WORDS**
Ship.

3 **BEEP BEEP!**
16. It appears six times in the units display, and ten times in the tens display.

4 **OFF LINE**
2, 5 and 18.

5 **ON GUARD**

6 **SECRET SEVEN**
Sausage.

7 BRUSH STROKES

19.

8 MIND THE GAP

All.

9 QUARTERBACK

```
      S O U P
      O G R E
      U R G E
  S L A P E E K I N D
  L O V E     I D E A
  A V O W     N E A R
  P E W S H E D A R K
      H I V E
      E V I L
      D E L L
```

10 SPLITZER

Heart/Liver.

11 TRIANGLE TEST

25.

12 HONEYCOMB

1. Pirate 2. Guards 3. Rugged 4. Murder
5. Summer 6. Rivets.
The inner circle spells TAURUS.

13 BACK WORDS

Pay ★ Yap.

(14)

MORE OR LESS

The number of hours in three days (72) is more than five and a half dozen eggs, 66.

(15)

ADDER

Ear + Wig = Earwig.

(16)

CREATURE CODE

1. Rat 2. Parrot 3. Panda

(17)

LINKS

Port.

(18)

SECRET SEVEN

Bowlers.

(19)

PICTURE GALLERY

Portrait number 11.

(20)

GIVE ME FIVE

1. First 2. Shell 3. Yacht 4. Storm
5. Torch 6. Pedal 7. Field 8. Three.
The word made is RECORDER.

21

CARD TRICK
The word RAW, reads WAR backwards.

22

LOTS OF SPOTS

S	P	O	T
P	A	V	E
O	V	A	L
T	E	L	L

O	D	D	S
D	R	O	P
D	O	D	O
S	P	O	T

I	S	L	E
S	P	O	T
L	O	A	N
E	T	N	A

23

TOP TEN
Ten. This completes the word extend.

24

WHAT'S NEXT
P. Letters are in alphabetical order,
with two missed out at each move.

25

ANIMAL–FILL
Ant completes the word panther.

26

TREE SURGERY
1. Bark 2. Roots 3. Branch 4. Leaf 5. Trunk.

27

SPLITZER
Eagle/Goose.

28

BLOCKS

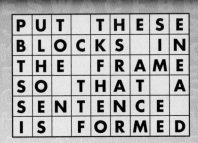

P	U	T		T	H	E	S	E
B	L	O	C	K	S		I	N
T	H	E		F	R	A	M	E
S	O		T	H	A	T		A
S	E	N	T	E	N	C	E	
I	S		F	O	R	M	E	D

29

ON LINE

Computer.

30

NICE MICE

1. Mice 2. Rice 3. Race 4. Face 5. Fare
6. Fire 7. File 8. Mile.

31

LINKS

Whale.

32

ON TARGET

17 + 24 + 39 = 80.

33

AFTER–WORDS

Line.

34

NUMBER-RING

28. 5 is added each time.

SECRET SEVEN
Bedroom.

PAIRS
2 and 5.

MIND THE GAP
Bat.

MORE OR LESS
The number of sides in four octagons, 32, is more than the sides in nine triangles, 27.

BACK WORDS
Pit * Tip.

SNAKES ALIVE
1. Adder 2. Cobra 3. Boa.

HAPPY BIRTHDAY
Jennifer's birthday is 31st December. The information would have been true on 1st January.

42

NATIONWIDE
1.Peru 2.Spain 3.Nepal 4.Yemen.

43

ADDER
Leg + End = Legend.

44

FACE FACTS
Polly.

45

SECRET SEVEN
Lobster.

46

NIGHT SIGNS
1. Owl 2. Deer 3. Bat 4. Possum.

47

MIND THE GAP
Pal.

48

LINKS
Bow.

49

BACK WORDS
Pot * Top.

50

ON THE MAP
Map C.

51

SQUASHED SANDWICHES!
1. Cheese 2. Tuna 3. Chicken 4. Turkey
5. Ham.

52

SECRET SEVEN
Carpets.

53

3D

54

PATTERN PLAY
No 3. The other patterns have the same
features in the same order.

55

ADDER
Fat + Her = Father.

56

STARGAZER
1. Flan 2. Foam 3. Flow 4. Wolf 5. Farm
6. Warn.

COMPUTER CODE
1. Computer   2. Mouse.

MIND THE GAP
Sit.

LEMON-AID
13 times.

AFTER–WORDS
Word.

ROUNDABOUT

62

LINKS
Chest.

63

EUROPEAN CAPITALS
1. Madrid 2. Paris 3. Athens 4. Rome
5. London 6. Berlin.

64

FRUITY
Peach. Take the letters PE (half of PEAR),
A (middle of GRAPE) and CH (one third
of CHERRY).

65

WHAT AM I?
Table.

66

MORE OR LESS
The number of days in May doubled is 62,
which is more than the 52 fortnights that are
in two years.

67

ALPHA-NUMBERS
1. Eleven 2. Eight 3. Twelve 4. Thirty
5. Fourteen.

68

SPLITZER
Canoe/Yacht.

69

FAST TRACK
A Tom ran 200 m and finished third.
B Rachel ran 400 m and finished last.
C Sarah ran 100 m and finished first.
D Robin ran 800 m and finished second.

70

BACKWORDS
Rat * Tar.

71

IN THE MIDDLE
1. L 2. E 3. M 4. O 5. N. LEMON

72

YOUR DEAL
5, 6, 7 and 8.

73

COMPU-COMMAND
Open.

74

MOONS
They are both the same size.

75
TOP TEN

Nine. This completes the word feminine.

76
NUMBER-RING

288. Each number is doubled.

77
ADDER

Off + Ice = Office.

78
NUMBER FIT

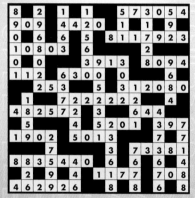

79
FACE FACTS

Timothy.

80
AFTER–WORDS

Time.

81
DOMINOES
Five dots. All the dominoes have nine dots.

82
MIND THE GAP
Low.

83
SECRET SEVEN
Capsule.

84
TRI-PATH
Path C. It contains eight triangles.

85
SIDEWAYS
The number of sides in three rectangles, 12, is more than the 10 sides in two pentagons.

86
LASSO

87

ORANGE PEEL
1. Range 2. Rang 3. Rag 4. Gear 5. Anger.

88

LINKS
Blue.

89

SPLITZER
Brick/Stone.

90

MUSIC BOX
Saxophone.

91

ADDER
For + Get = Forget.

92

WHAT'S NEXT?
J for June. They are the first letters of months of the year.

93

MIND THE GAP
Eat.

94

HANDY

14.

95

SECRET SEVEN

Chariot.

96

BLOCKBACK

Z	Y		S	Q	U	I	D
E	X	I	T		U		R
B		E		T	E	P	I	D
R	O	L	L		N		S
A		D	A	N	C	E		O
	S		W		H	A	L	F
S	T	A	Y	S		G		T
	E		E		F	L	E	E
S	W	O	R	D		E		N

97

BACK WORDS

Raw * War.

98

ROULETTE

99 AFTER–WORDS

Bone.

100 CENTURY

Yes. It will take 200 seconds to light them all. Each candle burns for three minutes – that's 180 seconds.

101 BACK WORDS

Yam * May.

102 ABC

Line 5.

103 SECRET SEVEN

Couples.

104 HAPPY FAMILIES

Eight. Two parents, five daughters and one son.

105 MIND THE GAP

For.

106

FACE FACTS

Fiona.

107

AFTER–WORDS

Day.

108

ADDER

Kid + Nap = Kidnap.

109

LINKS

Ski.

110

A SLICE OF LIME

Lime, Iron, Mood, Ends.
Glad, Lilo, Also, Doom.

111

NUMBER-RING

85. 1 is taken away, then 2, then 3, then 4, then 5.

112

PICK A WORD

TOOTH. The shape of the letters is the link. Each letter in each word is symmetrical – the left half is a mirror image of the right half.

113

CUBA

No 3.

114

ALPHA-SEARCH
Zebra.

115

LOTSA LEGS
35.

116

SPLITZER
Truck/Train.

117

ALL CHANGE
1. Slave 2. Shave 3. Shove 4. Shore
5. Chore 6. Chord.

118

MATCHING WORD
Running.

119

BACK WORDS
Draw * Ward.

120

PYRAMID

WHAT'S NEXT?
S. They are the first letters of days of the week.

SECRET SEVEN
Cutlery.

RHYMER
Heart.

ON LINE
Mouse.

AFTER-WORDS
Side.

BLANKS
48 goes inside the triangle. 16 goes outside. All the numbers are doubled with each triangle.

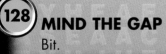

ADDER
Kit + Ten = Kitten.

MIND THE GAP
Bit.

129 MIRROR IMAGE

The L from CORRECTLY.

130 ON SONG

S	O	N	G
O	V	A	L
N	A	M	E
G	L	E	E

H	I	S	S
I	N	T	O
S	T	U	N
S	O	N	G

131 FACE FACTS

Charlie.

132 TOP TEN

One. This completes the word anyone.

133 MIDDLE MOVES

1. Cot Cut 2. Icy Ivy 3. Hit Hot 4. Stall Still
5. Chapter Chatter.

134 LINKS

Shell.

135 TRUE OR FALSE

Boy 1 is Carl Angel. He tells the truth.
Boy 2 is Andy De Villes, who lies.
Boy 3 is Bob De Villes, who lies.

136 SPLITZER

Attic/Floor.

137 NUMBER-RING

243. Numbers are multiplied by 3.

138 BACK WORDS

Deer * Reed.

139 AFTER–WORDS

Down.

140 SECRET SEVEN

Actress.

141 3-4-5

142 ADDER

Moo + Red = Moored.

G	R	A	N	D		D	U	V	E	T
L		N		I	C	E		I		A
O	U	N	C	E		E	X	C	E	L
O		U		T	I	P		A		L
M	E	L	T		N		A	R	M	Y
N		E	L	D	E	R		E		
I	D	E	A		E		M	I	N	D
N		N		A	X	E		D		W
C	I	V	I	C		A	L	I	V	E
U		O		H	A	S		O		L
R	H	Y	M	E		T	O	T	A	L

143 MIND THE GAP

Ram.

144 OH BOY!

1.Dean 2.Ernest 3.Dennis.

145 TOP OF THE HEAP

Light blue, Dark blue, Yellow, Purple, Black, Red, Green.